# Etiquette: A Necessity In the Workplace and Beyond

## A Business Etiquette Handbook For Professionals

*Foreword by*
**Dr. Tina Dupree**

Cover Photo by Darran Hill

Published by
Emerge Publishing Group, LLC
Riviera Beach, FL
www.emergepublishers.com

Printed in the United States of America

# Table of Contents

**Dedication**

**Foreword by Dr. Tina Dupree**

# Dedication

To my beloved mom, Mrs. Baby Harrysingh, now 91 years old for the selfless love and tremendous support you gave me in all my endeavors. You have always bolstered me, giving me new life when I seemed to wane and spiritual sustenance when tasks seemed insurmountable. You have always made my world a brighter place and I am eternally grateful. All my love now and always.

To my beloved sister, the late Betty Harrysingh, who inspired me to include Etiquette Practice in everyday life, I am forever grateful.

To my sisters, Pryma Myna & Tara, thanks for your love and inspiration.

To my dearest brothers, Dr. Ranjit Singh and Kamaljit Singh, You are my mentors and you have always supported me and given me strength.

I am forever grateful to my entire family.

# *An Expression of Gratitude*

My sincere appreciation to Dr. M. Tina Dupree of Motivational Training Center LLC for her tireless dedication in helping me to get this project completed. She kept me motivated during the entire process. Her first suggestion was for me to set goals on exactly what I wanted to write about and how the process of getting this done was most important. She helped me assemble this book and get it ready for the publisher. Dr. Dupree has a very busy schedule; she travels most of the week. When we met, it was as though I was her only client. She took the time and dedicated herself to researching my ideas, helping me with the manuscript, and she gave me suggestions on selecting the right publisher. I am grateful for her expertise and how she took her time and patience during this process.

Thank you Dr. M. Tina Dupree. Your experience in helping authors and your powerful motivation was instrumental in helping me get this book written and published.

# Thank You . . .

I would like to offer my thanks to the following individuals:

> **Jerry Nagee** is a life-long friend, who has mentored me and offered inspiration. She extended the hand of friendship when I first came to this country. I am forever grateful for the friendship that has been nourished with kindness, sympathy, and understanding.

Thanks to the following individuals who greatly contributed to the completion of this project. They provided valuable insight and information:

> **Dr. Neil Parsan**
> **Dr. Kushranie Maharajh**
> **Erica Williams**
> **Dr. Ron Peterson**

# Foreword

Proper business etiquette and social graces are expected in today's business and social world. But the problem is that most people are unaware in knowing exactly what to do. What fork to use at a formal dinner or exactly how to handle yourself at an important business event?  What about in the office? Your office cubical, the eating area in the office, or you may not be sure how to handle yourself if your boss invites you to his/her home for dinner.  In this book are answers to these and other questions regarding proper etiquette. This book gives excellent instructions and answers to your questions on how to conduct yourself in most business and social setting.

Ms. Shama Harrysingh, the Business Etiquette Coach, gives you plain and simple instructions on the "how tos" of every day etiquette practices. The information within these pages will help you to become an etiquette expert after learning from the Business Etiquette Expert.  Shama gives information and instructions as to how you should conduct yourself in the proper manner at the dinner table, in the office, and in everyday life where you must make a good impression.

Once you read this book and implement what has been written, you will find yourself more relaxed, confident, and never to be embarrassed again when you don't know what to do at a formal dinner, or attending an important meeting with top executives, or out with your friends in business or pleasure or any type of business or social setting.

**Dr. Tina Dupree**
**Professional Speakers Network**
**www.tinadupree.com**

*Chapter 1*

## INTRODUCTION TO
## ETIQUETTE 101

This book is written to help you improve your business and social skills. Being in the business arena for many years, I have discovered that some professionals lack the skills I will be presenting to you for a successful career. These skills will help you build a successful career, elevate you in the business world, gain self-confidence, and self-esteem.

A doctorate or any education is great. It is good to be smart but you need good etiquette to be impressive and successful. Two of the easiest and shortest words in the English Dictionary are the most difficult for us to say. How often do we forget or think that we should not say "please" or "thank you." When someone holds the door for you, or does a favor for you, say "Thank you." Please and Thank You should be effortless and spontaneous.

Good manners are a commodity no one can take or steal from you. It will never harm, only promote you. Good manners are timeless; they are never outdated.

Your behavior tells who you are–how you walk, speak, sit, and dress. Good posture defines your character. People judge you by your mannerisms, polished or unpolished.

You always want to look polished, so let's get started in our quest to be polished professionals.

# *Chapter 2*

## HISTORY OF ETIQUETTE

I shall give you some background (history) of etiquette procedures that will help you in your professional and social lives. As you read this book, I can hear you saying, "Shama, I did not know that." The numerous comments I received from people compelled me to write this book.

Good manners have been practiced for centuries. It started with simple rules in the homes and became part of our daily lives. These rules were guidelines and were treated seriously. They were a form of discipline for families. In ancient times, people took manners seriously.

Etiquette started in the sixteenth and seventeenth centuries by Ptah-Hotep, a great philosopher, who wrote the first book on etiquette during the fifth Egyptian Dynasty between 35-80 BC - 36 BC. He wrote a set of rules for his sons and said that all wise men should convey those rules to their sons.

> "Manners are a sensitive awareness of the feelings of others. If you have that awareness, you have good manners, no matter which fork you use.
>
> ~Emily Post

# Chapter 3

# BUSINESS ENVIRONMENT

## Business Settings

Everyone should feel comfortable in a healthy, clean, and neat working environment.

Your work area should differentiate between home and office. You should avoid bringing your home to the office. This includes bringing your personal life and problems into the workplace. What may seem appropriate to you may appear to be clutter to your co-workers. It is also very unprofessional to bring your personal business to the workplace. Everyone has problems but it can cause uncomfortable situations in the workplace if your personal business starts to become gossip.

## Business Speech

When speaking at work or in social business settings, avoid obscene language, such as profanity, inappropriate, or embarrassing words. For example: avoid using words like, "you fool,' "dumb," negative comments about co-worker's attire, religion, customs, beliefs, culture, racial slurs or sexual orientation. Comments such as these may be hurtful to others and you should eliminate these from your vocabulary completely. By using inappropriate terms, you may be liable and can contribute to legal action against you or your company.

Avoid negative words and the manner in which you speak. Instead of saying, "I don't know," make a suggestion. Use positive words and body language. Make eye contact to show that you are attentive. Use words of acknowledgement such as "absolutely," "definitely," "May I help you?" Always be polite and professional.

## Office Decor

Never over-decorate your office or work space with too many inappropriate frills. Decorations or personal items should be simple and professional. Check with management for Policies and Procedures regarding what is allowed in your office or work space. Too many plants, photographs, teddy bears, or other personal items such as knick-knacks may appear as clutter and very unattractive. Take into consideration that you share your office and what may be good to you may not be nice to other co-workers, visitors, and customers/clients. Before leaving the office, it is a good habit to leave your desk the way you would like for it to look when you return.

## Collections/Donations

Some companies allow employees to participate in donations for sports, football pools, birthday gifts, charities, cake or candy sales, or other types of collections. Always respect your co-workers. Some may not want to participate or may not have the money to help. Collections/donations should not be too expensive or too often. Remember, the company's policies should always be followed. Find out if collections/donations are allowed.

## Kitchen Etiquette

Food smells good and is sometimes inviting while other times offensive to others. Please confine food items and eating to the kitchen or designated areas. In some cases, it is acceptable to eat at your desk (if the company allows) or if you are unable to leave your desk. Don't take advantage of the situation; be reasonable.

It is a good idea to have lunch away from your desk. You have an opportunity to socialize with your co-workers, get to know them, stretch your legs, and relax. No one wants to see a dirty plate or smell food at your desk.

Please be considerate when eating in the office or at a social setting. Some foods make loud sounds when chewing. It is rude to make loud noises when eating. Eating and chewing can be done politely. Unless you have a medical problem, please take notice of how you eat in public.

Never pick, floss or try to clean your teeth at the table or in public. Do not walk around with a toothpick in your mouth. It is very un-appealing and unprofessional. Go to the rest room and clean your teeth.

Place food waste in the kitchen receptacle. The office waste basket should be used for office trash only and not your personal items. Remember, that the office kitchen is shared with your co-workers; be considerate. There are exceptions in some cases. However, please remember that you are at work, and not at home.

Clear the tables, wash the dishes, and leave the kitchen in order for the next person.

Do not leave containers in the refrigerator for several weeks to collect mold.  Clean the refrigerator and microwave after each use.

"Good manners is what enables a person to wait at the counter patiently and quietly for service—while the blabber mouth gets all the service."

~Anonymous

# *Chapter 4*

# TECHNOLOGY IN THE WORK PLACE

For many years, technology has made its way in today's world of business. The use of technology has become a major part of our daily work and personal lives. On www.cnet.com it is reported that 5 billion people worldwide own a cell phone and that even though we went through a major economic crisis, the demand did not decrease. Even more popular in the last couple of years is the Smart Phone.

# Communication

## The Phone:

In the case of the phone, there are some key factors to consider:

The use of technology in communications is making our personal and business lives better. No more business as usual with the use of all the modern, digital gadgets. A person does not need to be in the office to conduct business. It can be done from home with the use of our hi-tech gadgets. So whether we are in the office, on an airplane or sunning on a beach miles away from home, we can still conduct business.

A business owner today can conduct meetings, contact employees, send messages, send a fax while sitting in a restaurant, while traveling and many other ways to conduct business from a Smart Phone. Several years ago, this was unheard of. Today a PDA or i-Pad can do as much as a computer.

## Computers:

In the past, computers were used to communicate, but with limited access. However, the business owner today has global access and therefore, can do business, conduct meetings and video conferences worldwide. The global connection of the internet has allowed even the small business owner to increase sales.

Computers are used to make numerous tasks easier and more accessible for accounting, to provide information on almost any topic, including Geography, History, English, games, education, personal, or hundreds of others tasks. The possibilities are unlimited. The computer's keyboard has replaced the typewriter. Some of our young people today have never seen a typewriter. The keyboard on your Smart Phone or computer can self-correct, spell check and has numerous other functions to make it more convenient.

With the Smart Phone, you can store pictures, make a movie, send emails, surf the web, do extensive research, and many other functions too numerous to name. Technology has changed the way we communicate and do business with the world. Instant messaging is great for faster internal communications. There is little need for voice mail messages.

There are a wide variety of models and styles to choose from. So many in fact that it is sometimes hard to make a decision on which one is more suitable for your business.

## Desktop:

A Desktop computer is stationary and is usually on the desk or table in the office or at home.

## Laptop:

A Laptop also called notebook is smaller, lighter, compact and is quite convenient and mobile. It can be taken anywhere since it is battery operated. It is available in touch screen, digital and wireless; some of them are small enough to fit in your pocket.

## Tablet and iPad:

Becoming even more popular today are the Tablet and iPad. They have the same features as a computer in smaller and compact versions. However, its popularity has surpassed all expectations and is becoming the choice of millions of people, both young and old. When Apple announced the iPad a few years ago, they had no idea that it would become the technology of choice.

Because of this technology, it is predicted that APPLE could become the first trillion dollar company. (http://www.besttechinfo.com/apple-could-be-the-worlds-first-trillion-dollar-company/) So it is realistic to say that APPLE's iPad could replace the computer as we know it today.A Tablet PC is a cross between a notebook PC and a personal digital assistant (PDA). It's a flat-panel portable PC in the form of a slate.

Using technology saves time, money and is convenient. When we use this technology, we should adhere to the Etiquette or 'Netiquette'. There are guidelines and rules for users called "newbies" (newcomer or novice, especially an inexperienced user of the Internet or of computers in general).

## E-Mails:

It is recommended that you respond to e-mails within twenty-four hours, or at least acknowledge receipt of e-mail. This can be done by using an auto-responder. For a list of auto-responders, check the Internet and decide which is best for your use. Please ensure that proper grammar and correct spelling are used. Spelling and grammar can be checked immediately by using the spell check feature. Bad spelling and grammar give the recipient a bad impression of the writer and make a poor impression of your business.

Use pleasant language so when the reader reads your email, you would be visualized as a warm and friendly person. It is said that an email is the most misunderstood form of communication today. Tone even in writing is important. Also please note that emails can be saved forever, so be careful not to threaten or use improper language. It could work against you if needed as evidence in a court case or termination.

Avoid using all caps when writing for two reasons: capitals are difficult to read and it tells the reader that you are shouting or yelling in an angry tone. You want the reader to enjoy reading your e-mail. Lower case may take longer but creates a better layout and is the correct method.

When responding to emails re-read carefully before sending. Please be sure that your emails are forwarded to the right person. You may receive an e-email from a group but intend to reply to only one person. If you are not careful, you may unintentionally forward or reply to the entire group.

## Sending E-Mails

The use of e-mail in Corporate America is paramount; therefore, proper Business Etiquette is essential. Phone calls have become secondary to emails.

It cannot be emphasized enough how unethical it is to keep sending forwarded emails from one person to another several times for several days around the world using the same subject. In some cases it does not relate to the subject matter. The recipient may by-pass the email or delete it without reading it, thinking that it was read previously. Make sure the subject is appropriate for the message conveyed.

Always get permission to use someone else's computer. Always keep information of the company and its employees confidential.

Do not mix business with pleasure or personal matters. Do not abuse work times and privileges. Avoid sending IM's or e-mails to co-workers in the same work area unless it is absolutely necessary. Get up and stretch your legs; a little exercise will not hurt you. Walk over to the co-worker and personally give your message. Office gossip is definitely inappropriate and can cause conflict among employees.

Do not forward an e-mail unless it specifically applies to the person you are sending it to. If you must send or forward the same e-mail to a group of contacts, you can do so only when you put their e-mail addresses in the BCC: field to protect their privacy. Use the Cc: and BCC: features prudently by only including e-mail addresses that "need to know" the content of the e-mail. Do not use these options for e-tattling purposes; it is considered unethical and unprofessional. This will help to avoid problems.

It is a good habit to edit e-mails to remove any text that is irrelevant to the ongoing conversation.

Take the time to make sure that your sentences are complete, capitalized and include proper grammar, spelling, and punctuation. This goes for Twitter and Facebook as well. Educated professionals communicate in a professional manner regardless of venue (or device).

Making these efforts will go a long way to certify that communicating is easy and reliable while having the added benefit of helping to avoid any misunderstandings.

Some other *Best Practices* for e-mails are:

- Keep messages brief and to the point.

- Never criticize via e-mails. E-mail messages live forever.

- Do not send an unannounced large attachment of any kind without permission.

- Always read emails carefully before sending.

- Do not post e-mails that were sent to you privately for any reason in a public forum or forward them to a third party without the original sender's permission. Those who you forward business e-mails to that were intended for your eyes only will know this is poor behavior and that you are not to be trusted.

- Be very respectful about how you use your employer's technology resources understanding they are paying the bills and you are on their time.

- Do not assume any level of privacy while using company equipment, connectivity or e-mail resources.

- Refrain from formatting e-mails with colored text, bolding and/or italics because it does not look professional. Do not over-emphasize statements; they can give the recipient the wrong impression.

- Ensure that the *Subject* field will include a brief and concise description of the content. Modify or change the Subject field when necessary to better display what the e-mail contains when a conversation has moved off the original topic.

Remember, your business e-mail activity is all about forming relationships and "communicating with the knowledge, understanding and courtesy," not about abuse. Keep in mind that once an e-mail is sent, it cannot be erased.

Use it to your advantage and build strong business relationships.

Manage the flow of e-mails; do not let them overcrowd your mail folder.

Delete what you do not need while reading. Overflow may slow down the System; you may miss reminders or meetings scheduled. You can also prioritize your mail, example: urgent and next day.

## Technical Do's & Don'ts:

Mr. David Gurteen, an independent Knowledge Management Consultant, speaker, and facilitator gives the following Do's and Don'ts regarding electronic communication etiquette.

I do believe however that there is a single principle–that is one of Trust. Electronic communication should be used to build trust–not to destroy it.

- **do not** criticize or blame

- **do not** be manipulative

- **do not** be arrogant

- **do not** discuss emotional issues

- **do not** reply in the heat of the moment

- **do not** ignore messages to which a reply is needed

- **do not** breach confidentiality

- **do not** overload the system with unnecessary messages

Simply stop and think before sending a message. Be aware and remain conscious.

But there is more. There is the need to build trust–to make deposits in people's emotional bank accounts. This is the important bit that so frequently is overlooked. Building blocks include:

- **responding** in a timely manner

- **thanking** publicly

- **informing** people

- **apologizing** publicly

- **demonstrating** personal integrity

- **replying** promptly even to say no

- **praising** people

- **supporting** people

- **giving** positive feedback

- **keeping** promises

- **being** honest, kind and courteous

## Blogging:

Blogosphere is a new and exciting internet pastime. It is a short internet service which allows people to give their opinion on a particular theme that is being blogged.

It is important to read and follow the rules before blogging.

## Tweeting:

Another popular means of social networking, like all other means of Social networking, always follow guidelines.

"You should only follow people who you trust, you think are interesting, or that you learn from," says <u>Jeremiah Owyang</u>.

- Don't be offended if someone decides not to follow you back.

- Contents should be 140 words or less

- Decide if you want to keep it personal or business

- If business, you may benefit from it.

## Facebook:

- Do not tweet or visit Facebook on business time unless those activities are specifically part of your job description.

- Familiarize yourself with your employer's policies in order to do your job as expected.

Good manners are just a way of showing other people that we have respect for them.

~Bill Kelly

# Chapter 5

## SOCIAL GRACES

Customize your time. It is rude to be late. The first part of a class, meeting or any function is always the most important segment. Make it a habit to arrive fifteen minutes early for all appointments. In some cases, being late may be unavoidable and may be acceptable.

At a business dining, when the host or hostess arrives he or she should check the dining table to make sure that everything is in order, including the seating and décor.  The table should be decorated simply with a small centerpiece so that the guests can see the host or hostess and other guests visibly.

Guests who arrive before the host/hostess should wait in the lounge until other guests arrive.  They should not order until everyone arrives.  They should introduce themselves and get acquainted with each other.  After cocktails, the host/hostess seats the guests.  In some cases, the guests names are placed at their respective place.  I have been to functions where guests changed the name cards.  This is not a good idea. Seating was arranged carefully and with good reasoning.  Sitting next to someone you do not know is for you to get acquainted with that person.  Sometimes, a male is seated next to a woman or a young person next to an old person. No one takes their seat before the host.

Do not bring cocktail glasses to the dining table.  Because the table is already set, it may become crowded to place purses on the table.

Place purses on your lap or on the floor. Cell phones should be on vibrate. If you have to use your phone, excuse yourself and go outside. Women should walk to chairs from right. Men should sit after women.

Table setting can be formal or informal and menu is planned accordingly.

## **Utensils**

Use the utensils further away from the plates. For example: Formal dining may have a place setting to include more than one fork or more than one knife. Start with the knife and fork that are furthest away from the plate.

A table cloth extending 10–15 inches past the edge of the table should be used for formal dinners, while placemats may be used for breakfast, luncheon, and informal suppers.

Modern etiquette provides the smallest numbers and types of utensils necessary for dining. Only utensils which are to be used for the planned meal should be set. Even if needed, hosts should not have more than three utensils on either side of the plate before a meal. If extra utensils are needed, they may be brought to the table along with later courses.

Candlesticks, even if not lit, should not be on the table while dining during daylight hours.

Men's and unisex hats should never be worn at the table.

Do not use your phone at the table, or otherwise do anything distracting, such as read or listen to a personal music player. Unless you are alone, reading at the table is permitted only at breakfast. If an urgent matter arises, apologize, excuse yourself, and step away from the table so your conversation does not disturb the others.

It is accepted that you may place your elbows on the table as long as you do not rest weight upon them. Historically it had been rude to place your elbows on the table but this formally changed in the mid-nineties.

- The fork may be used either in the "American" style (use the fork in your left hand while cutting; switch to right hand to pick up and eat a piece; this is common practice in the US) or the European "Continental" style (fork always in left hand).

- Leave the napkin on the seat of your chair only if leaving temporarily. When you leave the table at the end of the meal, loosely place the used napkin on the table to the left of your plate.

**"Work etiquette"** is a code that governs the expectations of social <u>behavior</u> in a <u>workplace</u>, in a group or a <u>society</u>. Work etiquette tells the individual how to behave when dealing with situations in a working environment however trivial the situation is. Office etiquette in particular applies to co-worker interaction and communication with colleagues. There is no universal agreement about a standard work etiquette which may vary from one environment to another.

# Out of the Office Party Rules

Attending an office party? Don't check your professional reputation along with your coat. An office party gives you the opportunity to celebrate the holidays or other occasion with your co-workers. You should have fun, but be careful about having too good a time. Follow these tips and you'll be able to return to the office with your head held high.

1. **Don't Drink Too Much**

    Alcohol lowers your inhibitions and alters your judgment. It can make you do things you may regret. Even if you think you can handle your alcohol quite well, one mixed drink or a glass of wine at the office party should be your limit. Remember, perception is everything. You don't want to look like you're drinking too much, even if alcohol has little effect on you.

## 2. Don't Treat the Office Party like a Singles Bar

An office party gives you a chance to see another side of your co-workers. However, you shouldn't try to get to know any of them too well. Ignore your romantic instincts. Workplace romances—or worse, one night stands—can be disastrous.

## 3. Don't Flirt or Act in a Sexually Provocative Manner

Your flirting may be entirely innocent but the message it sends to your colleagues isn't innocent. If you want to be respected on a professional level, save this side of yourself for parties with friends.

## 4. Don't Wear Suggestive Clothing

Most importantly, this the age of 'facebook' and 'YouTube'. Before you turn around, everything will be on face book.

## Airline Etiquette for Professionals

Remember you are representing your company and should project a Professional image.

Avoid walking up to the ticket counter while you are on the phone. It only takes about three minutes to check out if all of your paperwork is complete.

It is rude to talk to the representative while you are on the telephone; you hold back the line and distract others in line.

Do not approach the counter with your ticket in your mouth; it is very unsanitary. Instead, put your ticket in your pocket.

Eating tables are not for changing diapers, the airplane has tables for changing diapers towards the lavatory. Passengers have to eat on those tables and they are not cleaned after every flight.

This has nothing to do with not liking babies. Babies are beautiful; everyone loves them.

When traveling, keep computer in a nice bag. Most laptops come with a convenient bag with different compartments. When on an airplane, do not spread your items all over, since there is limited space. Keep everything neat, and turn off devices when required. There is a reason why you are asked to do so; it may interfere with the airplane's communications system.

When reclining, remember, there is some one behind you. Also, remember to share the arm rest equally.

If you would like to change seats and sit in a vacant seat, wait until the flight takes off or check with the flight attendant.

The overhead bin is shared by three people in some cases. Be considerate of fellow passengers and flight attendants who get blamed when they cannot find room for their luggage.

Passengers pack their luggage heavy and expect the flight attendants to carry it for them; it is not their job to carry your luggage except in the case of a disabled or elderly person.

Safety Regulations dictate that they are only supposed to help you guide the bag.

## Body Language and Business Etiquette

Body language plays a major role when communicating. It is important to pay attention to your body language. Although, non-verbal, it is very effective especially in job interviews and business.

It is a good idea to know what body language signifies so we can use it properly and effectively to convey the right message.

When you stand, keep your back straight, middle section in alignment with your back, shoulders back, and head up. This posture connotes comfort with yourself and ease in the situation.

Do not fold your arms or put them in your pockets; it shows that you are withdrawn or uneasy.

## Sitting

Always sit properly, sit upright with back straight, with legs in front of you or crossed. Normally, women don't cross their legs, but men are allowed. Avoid jiggling your knee, which is a sign of nervousness (and can be pretty annoying to people sitting near you).

## Hands

Being too dramatic with your hands can be annoying. Keep your hands relaxed.

Some people talk with their hands; others stand with their hands glued to their sides. Most people just move them all over without any meaning.

Using your hands can be effective sometimes, aggressive sometimes, and irrelevant most of the time. Use your hands to convey what you really want to say. Controlling your hands takes effort and willpower. Monitor your hand movements. Avoid making sweeping, cappuccino-clearing gestures during meetings. If you have to, sit on your hands.

## Head movements

Head movements communicate important information. Most people shake them for 'no' and 'yes'. Nodding in agreement can be immensely helpful to others. Too much nodding can be boring so avoid shaking your head too much..

## Facial expressions

Facial expressions are crucial in your repertoire of body language. This is the first part of your body someone looks at; you want to make sure you give out positive vibrations.

Smiles are important. They show warmth and acceptance.

If false, you look very unattractive.

- Likewise, frowns signal disagreement, disapproval, and sometimes anger. But they can also suggest hard thinking and focused concentration.

## Eye contact

Maintain eye contact when talking with others. Do not play with your hands or clean your fingernails while others are talking. When talking in a group, make eye contact with everyone; don't focus on only one person.

"Good manners will open the doors that a good education cannot."

~ Clarence Thomas

Here is a true etiquette story that I hope will put a smile on your face....

Did you hear about how good manners this week led to the purchase of a $319 million winning lottery ticket -- and how bad manners caused someone else to lose out?

The man who eventually bought the ticket was in line, and reached down to buy a Snickers bar. When he did, the person behind him cut in front of him, and bought a lottery ticket first.

The eventual winner didn't complain when the other person cut in front of him. He graciously let him go ahead of him. And he was rewarded in a big way. By waiting just one spot, he ended up with the winning ticket, worth $319 million.

So, if anyone ever tells you that etiquette isn't worth anything, you can reply that good etiquette is worth hundreds of millions of dollars, and bad manners can cost just as much.

Help the people in your community learn good manners, civility, and kindness. They might not win the lottery, but they will be set up for a lifetime of success and better relationships.          ~ Elena Neitlich 2011

# Chapter 6

## BUSINESS ATTIRE

The purpose of this Chapter is to establish rules and dress codes to help you improve your office image. If there are no written guidelines for dress code, employees will determine what they should wear, whether their perception is appropriate or inappropriate.

Working in the business arena for many years, I have noticed that some professionals lack the skills to dress appropriately for work.

Corporations want their employees to project a professional image by adhering to an established dress code. This will enable employees to represent the company and the brand in a more professional manner. Dress codes are important and the new business trend for a lot of major brands are now requiring their employees to wear company provided shirts with the company's printed logo.

The employee's appearance as a business professional on a daily basis, using a formal dress code will give your clients and customers a clear indication of professionalism.

## Dress to Impress

It is important to dress properly and appropriately for all business related matters. In today's business world, there are a variety of fashion choices. Some are trendy, simple and sophisticated. Create a look that makes you look smart and professional. What you wear depicts who you are in the eyes of the business world. Just as it is with technology, it is important to keep up with the constant changes in Business Fashions. The Queen of England is reported to have told Prince Charles, *"Dress gives one the outward sign from which people can judge the inward state of mind. One they can see, the other they cannot."* Clearly, what she was saying is that many people judge us by the way we dress.

Develop your own personal image but remain in the guidelines of professionalism. Each person is different and has different taste. Proper attire reveals your confidence and helps you look radiant.

## Formal Business

For both men and women, suits are ideal for a formal business setting. Depending on the season, choose solid colors. Always choose colors to enhance your complexion. Some colors look dull and make us appear depressed. We look stunning and feel vibrant in some colors. The appropriate colors can make us feel high-powered, energetic and on top of the world. Color should be based on your personality and complexion.

## COLORS:

Color affects the way we feel. It can affect our moods in either a positive or negative manner. The colors that we wear and surround ourselves with reflect our inner state of being.

### *Blues*

Blue has a large number of shades, and each conveys a different message. Choose your shade of blue based on the feelings you want to express, as well as your own skin tone and color.

### *Conservative Colors*

**Black** is another conservative color, but must be used wisely. For women, black blouses or pants are often acceptable and even expected at business meetings. For men, however, a black suit can some-

times portray an overwhelming serious-
ness, reminding your business associate of
a funeral or a black-tie ball instead of just
a business meeting. Consider sticking with
the dark gray or blue suits instead.

### *Brighter Colors*

Some brighter colors can be useful in
business situations, but much like black,
they must be worn with care. For instance,
color expert, Mary Giuseffi, suggests that
red can symbolize feelings of power,
focus, control and enthusiasm. She notes
that many political figures will wear red
ties when appearing on television to convey these emotions.

Giuseffi also suggests bright colors
like light green or yellow to convey opti-
mism, clarity and happiness.

Take care with these brighter colors,
however, that you are not overwhelming
your business associates. If you are inter-
viewing or presenting information, you do

not want your audience to be so distracted by your bright clothing that they miss what you are saying. Balance your colors, or use just a simple accent piece that can add personality to your navy or dark gray suit.

If you want to err on the side of caution, stick with conservative colors, to make sure you get your point across properly.

## Geographic and Climate Settings

In the winter, dark colors are preferable and you can mix and match accessories. Scarves are very popular for women in the Winter and can be worn in many different styles. Use scarves to enhance your looks and create a smart look. Avoid too much flashy jewelry.

In Spring and Summer, bright colors like red, yellow, and blue are more appropriate. You may also use lovely and simple jackets in light cotton fabrics to complement your look. It is fine to mix and match solids and patterns.

## Women

In general, women's clothing should not be too tight or too loose. If it is too tight, you may be uncomfortable, too loose may look sloppy. Clothes should be tailored and fitted for business.

A nice blouse worn with a skirt or pants is ideal and professional and adds a soft feminine touch to your appearance. Although, Management states business casual, it eliminates clothing which may be distracting or offensive, example: Shirts with slogans or writings not suitable for the office. Make use of the beautiful colors which will make you look sophisticated.

## Formal Business Attire

For women, a fitted suit jacket paired with a blouse is appropriate for a business casual workplace. Mix and match works well, for solid colors a nice brooch or scarf enhances your outfit. This is a crisp, professional look, but still appears relaxed with a more casual vibe. Costume jewelry is quite fashionable and can also be worn if is a simple piece. Simple accessories complement your outfit, giving it a rich look.

- Skirts should be knee-length or slightly above or below. Avoid extremes. A skirt more than two inches above the knee raises eyebrows and questions.

- Pants should break at the top of the foot or shoe. While Capri pants and their fashion cousins that come in assorted lengths from mid-calf to ankle are the latest trend, they are out of place in the conservative business environment.

- Blouses and sweaters provide color and variety to woman's clothing, but they should be appealing rather than revealing. Halters, deep V lines and short dresses may give the wrong impression.

- Dresses, skirts, skirts with jackets, dressy two-piece knit suits or sets, and skirts that are split at or below the knee are acceptable. Inappropriate slacks or pants include any that are too informal. This includes jeans, sweatpants, exercise pants, Bermuda shorts, short shorts, skorts, bib overalls, leggings, and any spandex or other form-fitting pants such as people wear for exercise or biking.

- Short, tight skirts that ride halfway up the thigh are inappropriate for work. Mini-skirts, shorts, sun dresses, beach dresses, and spaghetti-strap dresses are inappropriate for the office.

For tropical countries, choose cotton, linen, and silk fabrics which tend to breathe more than synthetics such as polyester. It is light and easier to clean.

## **Hosiery**

Keep an extra pair of stockings in your desk drawer unless the hosiery store is next door or just down the street from the office. Carry a bottle of clear nail polish in your purse to dab on snags and runs to stop them from spreading down your leg.

## **Shoes**

- Most people do not pay attention to their feet. Your feet are just as important as your face or the rest of your body. A low heel is more professional than flats or high heels. Quite fashionable now are pumps made popular by the Duchess of Cambridge. Neutral colors are appropriate for work.

- In spite of current fashion and the sandal rage, open-toed, flip flops or backless shoes are not office attire. Sandals are a safety hazard and many organizations do not allow them.

## Handbags

- Handbags should be in proportion to your size. Choose a bag with quality and neutral colors. Custom made Ostrich Crocodile is just as sophisticated.

- Don't put your entire household in your handbag. Just include the essentials–car keys, cell phone, compact, lipstick, a note book, and a pen. Sometimes you have everything in your pocket book and cannot find anything. It can be embarrassing and you may be looked at as a disorganized person.

## Briefcase

- Professionals should have a briefcase instead of carrying files in your hands.  It should be small and neat, preferably leather.

- Get one that will add elegance to your look.

## **Make Up**

The first thing people notice about you is your makeup.  Light makeup is recommended for the office; it is important to use the right shade.  Too much makeup can make you look gaudy, older and even like you are on the prowl. You don't want to send the wrong message. Keep makeup light and fresh. Heavy makeup under office lighting does not do any woman justice, in fact, if your office has fluorescent lighting any makeup you wear will appear heavier than it would under incandescent lighting.

Dark colored, bright red, and heavy lipstick is fine for evening events but keep lipstick colors pale and sheer for the office.

## Perfume

Perfume can trigger asthma and allergies in the people around you. Strong scents rarely appeal to anyone but the wearer. If you do wear scented products to work keep it as light as possible. If someone can smell you the second you enter a room, or your scent lingers in the air after you leave the room, you are wearing too much. Body mists come in tropical scents, are natural, refreshing, and ideal for the office

Remember that some employees are allergic to the chemicals in perfumes and makeup, so wear these substances with restraint and consideration for others.

No dress code can cover all contingencies so employees must exert a certain amount of judgment in their choice of clothing to wear to work. If you are not sure or have doubts about what is acceptable as formal business attire please ask your Supervisor, Manager or contact Human Resources.

## Business Casual

In a casual work setting, employees should wear clothing that is comfortable and practical for work, but not distracting or offensive to others. Any clothing that has words, terms, or pictures that may be offensive to other employees is unacceptable. Clothing that has the company logo is encouraged. Sports team, university, and fashion brand names on clothing are generally acceptable.

Business casual is very popular in today's business world and can be done with class, although casual. Corporations want their employees to project a professional and smart image thus, they establish a dress code to allow their employees to represent them and their products in a genuine manner.

The Company's employee objective in establishing a formal work dress code is to enable employees to project the professional image that is in keeping with the needs of clients and customers. Because our industry requires the appearance of trusted business professionals and we serve clients at our site on a daily basis, a more formal dress code is necessary for our employees. You must project the image of a trust-worthy, knowledgeable business professional for the clients who seek our guidance, input, and pro-fessional services.

Clothes should not be wrinkled; they should be neatly pressed and seamed if necessary.

## Formal Dress Code Guidelines

### Formal Dress Code – Men

Suits or Jackets well co-ordinated with shirts, ties, socks and shoes.

### Formal Dress Code –Women

Suits can be pants or skirts, again well-coordi-nated, not too revealing.

It is a good idea to have at least one blazer or sport coat.

**Business Casual; Men and Women**

**<u>Men</u>**

Your business casual wardrobe should include:

- Solid colors dress shirts including at least 2 white casual shirts in soft and relaxed fabrics such as denim, cotton and linen in various colors & patterns, at least 2 ties

- Sport shirts or Polo Shirts with collars

- A sweater

- Tailored trousers in year round fabrics

- Casual pants such as chinos (type of fabric)

- At least 2 pairs of leather shoes, 1 lace up and 1 loafer style

## Women

- Go for what's versatile. Buy quality vs quantity. Maintenance is important – blazers & coats should be dry cleaned

- If you decide to clean, read care instructions.

- Never wear shorts to the office

- Wear short sleeves only in Spring & Summer

- Never wear sleeveless blouses or dresses

- Choose lightweight material 100 % cotton for shirts

- Wear lightweight socks

- Pants made of light materials – cotton. Cotton-linen, poplins or chino.

- Popular ties:  Finest ties are made from silk that has been cut 'on the bias' —that is diagonally across the weave of the fabric.

- Some styles include the foulard, which features small prints such as dots, squares and tossed pin.

- The 'grenadine' is a slightly textured silk tie in which the weave of the fabric creates the pattern.

- Thin socks are dressy, thick socks are not.

- Small patterns on a sock are dressier than large patterns

- You can match socks to pant color but they should be lighter than the pant color.

- Attache Case - "Stuffable:" attaché cases works best for men, made of nylon, cotton or supple leather are lighter and more flexible and durable than traditional cases and work beautifully in a wide range of business situations. In addition, many have shoulder straps making them more comfortable to carry.

- Cell phone is not an article of clothing or a piece of jewelry or a bauble to be displayed on your belt or elsewhere, should be in your pocket or business case.

- Suits should be of natural and conservative colors. Usually black, charcoal, navy, dark brown or gray. A business suit should not be overly shiny, but more modest. It should also be either solid-colored or pinstriped.

- A suit should always be buttoned while standing. It is considered acceptable to unbutton a suit while sitting in a chair. A single-button suit is considered to be more leisurely, and it should be avoided in a business setting. A two-button suit should have either the top button or both buttons done up, a three button suit need only the top two buttoned, and a four-button suit should have the middle two buttoned.

### Shirt

The shirt you choose to wear with your suit should be woven and have a collar. It should be of solid color and lighter than that of your suit. The shirt should be a button-up with long sleeves. Cuff links are optional.

### Tie

The tie should be tied four-in-hand, half-Windsor (single) or full-Windsor(double) knot. The end of the tie should stop about at your belt. A striped tie should never be worn with a pin-striped suit. If wearing a solid suit, choose a tie of modest decoration.

*Socks and Shoes*

Socks should cover the calf and match the pants of the suit but be darker. They should be made of wool or cotton. Never wear a casual shoe with a suit; Oxfords and Derbies are most widely accepted.

Oxford is more formal shoes than Derby. For a more casual look, Derby shoes are great, perfect with jeans or chinos. (twill fabric made of 100 % cotton). These shoes are quite comfortable. You may wear shoes of your choice; they do not have to be designer shoes.

## Outside the Office

Many corporations require their employees to meet customers outside of the office, represent the company at a function or Trade show. Depending on the situation, attire can be formal or casual. It is important to check what is appropriate.

### Handkerchiefs – Men & Women

Handkerchiefs date back to ancient Rome when the Romans used them as props in theatres and the audience also waved kerchiefs at special games.

In the 16th century, wealthy women used them to cover their face to prevent germs. Later on Handkerchiefs were the main accessory for men and women; it became a fashion statement. Handkerchiefs come in different fashions, colors and materials, the most common for women are the lace and embroidery folded in a triangle. In addition to being a fashion accessory, it can be used to pat your face or if you have a cold. A woman's handkerchief usually has the initial of her first name.

Men's kerchiefs usually come in cotton and different colors. Most men prefer white with the initial of his last name.

Although, wearing a handkerchief is not as common today, it can be used by both men and women to give a polished look.

> "A highway is a road that can make bad manners fatal."
>
> ~ Anonymous

*Chapter 7*

# PROFESSIONAL TIPS
# FOR WOMEN

## Daily Tips Before you
## Leave Home

Before you leave for work or a social engage-
ment, examine yourself with your best friend–a
full length mirror. Look at yourself from the
front, back and sides from head to toe. Look at
every detail and make sure you look polished.

A few tips to help you with your daily grooming before leaving home which will give you self-confidence:

- Hair should be neatly combed and off your face

- Blend makeup, use lightly

- Finger nails should be well manicured and clean

- If nails are polished use neutral colors

- Teeth should be clean and sparkling

- Clothes should fit properly, not too tight or loose or short

- Knee length is fine

- Clothes should be wrinkle free

- Clothes should not be torn or stained

- Clothes and shoes should be color co-ordinated

- Use hosiery in neutral tones

- Do not use flashy jewelry

- Make sure clothes are color coordinated

- Respect everyone, walk tall

- Be positive

- You are the most elegant person on earth

- A nice bright smile and you are ready for the world

"Nothing is less important than which fork you use. Etiquette is the science of living. It embraces everything. It is ethics. It is honor."

~Emily Post

Treat everyone with politeness, even those who are rude to you - not because they are nice, but because you are.

~Author Unknown

*Chapter 8*

## COMMENTS FROM
## BUSINESS EXPERTS

### Good Business Etiquette
### Generates Loyal Clients

Business Etiquette spans a large spectrum from personal image to company branding. Personal image is very important for those who wish to get ahead in this competitive business environment. By dressing for success and insisting on high standards, you establish personal standards for yourself and your business. To fall below this standard is to develop a culture of insecurity, doubt and lack of confidence in you as a business person.

For those in the service industry, customer relations are of paramount importance. I have observed front office managers over the years and within a minute, I can easily identify those who are bad and counter-productive to a business, and those who will excel at promoting a business. Many clients who receive bad customer service, respond to it by not returning. Others may take the trouble to lodge a complaint with a manager, knowing that the likelihood of any changes in customer satisfaction or efficiency of service is very unlikely.

For the businesses that excel, it is very easy to see why. From the first point of contact with a receptionist, to a meeting with the CEO, there is a culture of efficiency, good customer service, and a friendly, helpful atmosphere which generates confidence, efficiency and good services. These qualities go a long way to generating client loyalty."

**Professor A. Ronald Peterson**

*South University*

*West Palm Beach, Florida*

\*\*\*

## Manners Maketh Man

Two of the worst things people can do denoting a complete lack of business etiquette:

1. To shake hands or converse with someone and not make direct eye contact tells the person:

   a) you're not interested in meeting me and

   b) you're not interested in what I have to say.

2. To text or check email at a dinner or head table - even worse, to talk on your phone is rude. If you have a phone call or urgent message, depending on how well you know the person, you CAN take it but only after excusing yourself and explaining that it is urgent. If you don't know the people well, you remove yourself from the setting

and do what you have to do, then return.

There are countless other examples I can offer: not standing when a lady approaches a dinner/lunch table. Not opening a door for a lady. Men getting off an elevator first, etc. The examples are legion, unfortunately. The younger generation—and even some of the older—would do well to remember that old adage: **manners maketh man.**

But then, as females, we wanted to be "equal," so what do we expect? We couldn't remember that *the hand that rocks the cradle, rules the world.* We wanted to be treated "the same." Well, we got it!

**Erica Williams Connell**
*Miami Director*
*The Eric Williams Memorial Collection*
   *Research Library, Archives & Museum*
*University of the West Indies, Trinidad*
   *and Tobago*

# The Importance of Business Etiquette

Business etiquette is important in many aspects of a professional's life. It is present at the time of first contact and expressed in the form of politeness, a firm handshake, neat dress, maintenance of eye contact and appearing engaged during conversations.

First impressions are important. Fidgeting, texting, or losing the train of conversation can indicate to a prospective client or employer that you are not interested in them. Another important part of business etiquette is timely follow-up post interview or meeting. This can be done by phone or email. All email correspondence in business must be done in a professional manner with appropriate heading, full sentences, and the presence of our contact information and the absence of extras, such as smiley faces or other non-business related icons.

In this age of electronics, it is also important to discuss mobile phone etiquette. Mobile phones should be turned to silence mode during meetings or when left at your desk if you work close to others. Texting to anyone (business related included) should be done when you are not in direct verbal conversation with others.

Finally, a note on international business etiquette: America is often known for a more casual, common sense approach to etiquette; however, many other countries can have very different rules and codes of behavior. This should be looked into prior to interactions with international clients.

In the business world, appropriate etiquette delineates a code of conduct that allows all individuals to interact civilly with one another. Learning this code will allow a professional more self-confidence as she encounters various business situations on the road to success.

**Dr. Kushranie Maharaj**
*South Florida Bone Marrow/*
*Stem Cell Transplant Institute*
*Boynton Beach*

# CONCLUSION

Those who follow what is set forth in this book will be successful in both their business and social life. It is about doing the right thing and being mindful of your fellow workers. The legendary Queen of Soul, Aretha Franklin stated it best: "R-E-S-PE-C-T, find out what it means to me R-E-S-P-E-C-T". Aretha Franklin's hit signature song is ranked # 5 on Rolling Stone's list of "The 500 Greatest Songs of All Time."

As one can tell, a little respect goes a long way. Respect in corporate America starts with the individual employee, which involves the application of basic courtesies that are called "Business Etiquette." It is a standard that seems to be forgotten.

Many times we are asked the question, "What happened to good old fashioned values?" Is it that we don't care anymore? Are we so wrapped up in our own world that we forget our manners? I have made an attempt in this book to re-visit good old-fashioned values.

## What is "Business Etiquette"?

My personal definition is "the composition of the best and proper manners, courtesy, and respect towards others and self. It's the adherence of a value system; also, it's a refined and delightful presence in social gatherings. "

I will conclude by re-iterating five areas I think are very important:

1) **The Office** (Cubicle / Private Office)– It doesn't matter if you work for a fortune 500 company or a mom and pop company, basic Business Etiquette should always apply. Workers should never infringe on others work space.

   • Keep noise level down at your desk.

   • Do not wear strong perfume.

   • Do not touch anyone's body part including a handshake if not offered.

2) **Professional Appearance** – The dot com companies have changed the way we use to dress. We as a nation have gone from business casual Fridays, to dress down Fridays and now just dress down Monday thru Friday. What happen to the dress code? Personally I believe attitudes reflect the way you look and sometimes feel. It is never proper "Business Etiquette" to wear flip flops, miniskirts, excessive face piercings, tank tops, etc... An office is not a Dance Club or a day at the beach. Always be mindful, not to distract your co workers. Rule of Thumb - Always become familiar with your company's "Dress Code".

3) **The phone** – Before dialing out, it is imperative to be prepared before calling out. It is vital to represent one's self as the ultimate professional / expert, which is effectively achieved with preparation

regarding subject matter! Here are some "Best Practices":

- Be prepared for rebuttal / resolve

- Smile while dialing

- Speak clearly

- Identify yourself

- Before placing a caller on hold, ask for permission first and thank them.

- It is better to return a call than to keep someone on hold too long. If the phone rings back to you, you've kept them on hold too long.

- Inbound and outbound calls are to be returned promptly. Always deliver on your promises.

- Never permit the phone to ring more than three times.

- Always use a pleasant, accommo-
dating, and friendly tone.

- Never interrupt the person while
he/she is talking to you.

- Avoid confrontational / argument
with a caller.

4) **Email** - The use of e-mail in Corporate
America is paramount; therefore, proper
Business Etiquette is essential. A matter of
fact phone calls has become secondary to
emails. As an executive I'm always
amazed and shocked by with people's
improper use of email; therefore, I will
share some suggestions.

- **Never criticize via email!** E-mail
is a terrific way to commend
someone or praise them. It is not
an appropriate medium for criti-
cism. Chances are, you will simply offend the other person, and
they will miss your point. These

kinds of conversations are usually better handled face-to-face or, if necessary, over the phone.

- **Don't reply in anger.** This does not serve your purpose or your long-term interests. The wrong response can destroy relationships faster than just about anything you can do. If you need to vent, then write the message, and delete it. Never use profanity!

- **Reply in a timely manner,** otherwise you will slowly damage your reputation and integrity.

- **Never write in ALL CAPS, as it is considered screaming/yelling.** Always conclude with **a signature containing your contact information.** This is simple courtesy for those who will be receiving your messages, so they will know who sent the message.

- **Always use spell-check.** Remember that you are representing yourself and your company. Misspelled words are just too easy to correct. Make sure yours is turned on.

- Before sending, remember that company e-mail isn't private. You have no legal protection. Anyone with sufficient authority can monitor your conversations on company-owned servers.

5) **Superiors** – respect both the person and the position.

   Respect works both ways when it comes to the superior and subordinate relationship. Both positions are EQUAL, when it comes to R-E-S-P-E-C-T. Most company policies and procedures clearly spell out the responsibilities of subordinates, but most often there is a lot of gray, as it applies to the superior. I will attempt to add some color .

- Often times the superior plays a dual role of being both superior and subordinate, in this case there's always a reminder of how to treat his or her subordinate. When it comes to respect, the best practice for the superior is to take on an attitude of equal in RESPECT and partners TEAMWORK, as oppose to "I'm the boss!" The superior works together by provide all the necessary tools to serve the subordinate. Yes serve! The best superiors are "Servant Leaders!" Servant leaders ask more than demand. Servant leaders are exemplary in action.

- The subordinate is to take on the attitude of respect for the leadership role/position. The subordinate is to work in excellence as a follower, in hopes to be recognized someday for promotion. Great followers are promoted quicker than conceited individuals.

• The superior and subordinate role should be collaborative endeavor, understanding mission and expectation within environment. One of my favorite quotes state "the more power over others you surrender, the more power you gain through others to move your organization forward."

When applied correctly, Business Etiquette will show you to be approved as someone who can be trusted to represent your team/department/company. The proper 'Business Etiquette' will foster a healthy work environment and create an exemplary culture. The most important thing to remember is the great manners that mama taught you! Co- workers deserve R-E-S-P-E-C-T!

# About the Author

Shama Harrysingh has a Bachelor of Arts Degree in Economics from the University of Winnipeg, Canada where she resided for many years.

She was born in Trinidad, West Indies. She is a Realtor and Licensed Mortgage Broker in the state of Florida where she made her home after migrating from Canada. She is a Certified Etiquette Coach, Certified Image Consultant, and a Certified Professional Communicator (CPC).

Shama is a former member of the Humanitarian Society of Boca Raton, Florida, and current Public Relations Officer of Divali Nagar South Florida, Inc. Shama works extensively as a volunteer in her community including the Annual Sunfest, South Florida's largest Waterfront festival of music and the arts, and the 44th Super Bowl held in Miami in 2010. At present, she volunteers as a teacher of literacy classes/Mentor in the City of Boca Raton.

Through Shama's volunteering, she enhanced services and expanded programs for the benefit of the citizens, employees and visitors of Boca Raton. The city honored her during National Volunteer Week with a Proclamation by Mayor Susan Whelchel during the 16th Annual Recognition Breakfast and Awards Ceremony.

As a philanthropist, Shama gave back to her community by producing two radio programs in the South Florida area on WAVS and WSHR radio stations.

Shama has traveled widely. She has visited Europe, the Caribbean, South America and India thus gaining the breadth of experience that translates into effective interpersonal skills complementing her work with the multicultural community she serves with dedication and profound commitment.

www.ingramcontent.com/pod-product-compliance
Lightning Source LLC
Chambersburg PA
CBHW070851280326
41934CB00008B/1391